BASEBALL

Junior Sports

Morgan Hughes

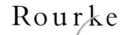

Rourke
Publishing LLC
Vero Beach, Florida 32964

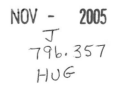

www.rourkepublishing.com

PHOTO CREDITS: Cover, p 6, 7, 9, 12, 15, 18, 28 Photos.com; p 5, 11 Natalie Behring-Chisolm/Getty; title page, p 13 Jed Jacobsohn/Getty; p 16 Exra Shaw/Getty; p 19 Todd Warshaw/Getty; p 20 Jonathan Daniel/Getty; p 22 Elsa/Getty; p 23 Tony Duffy/Getty; p 25 Doug Pensinger/Getty; p 26 Stephen Chernin/Getty; p 29 Tom G. Lynn/Getty

Title page: *There is nothing like a home run, whether it's Barry Bonds chasing down the all-time record or a little leaguer smacking one out of the park.*

Editor: Frank Sloan

Library of Congress Cataloging-in-Publication Data

Hughes, Morgan, 1957-
  Baseball / Morgan Hughes.
      p. cm. -- (Junior sports)
  Includes bibliographical references (p.   ) and index.
  ISBN 1-59515-188-5
  1. Baseball--Juvenile literature. I. Title. II. Series: Hughes, Morgan, 1957- Junior sports.
  GV867.5.H86 2004
  796.357--dc22
                                    2004009368

Printed in the USA

CG/CG

TABLE OF CONTENTS

AMERICA'S SPORT

Baseball is more than just a popular sport for boys and girls. And though it's part of the fabric of America its popularity is worldwide. The annual Little League World Series sends teams from Asia, Latin America, Canada, Mexico, Europe, and the Caribbean.

The catcher waits, the batter swings...is it a strike, a home run? That's baseball!

A baseball field—or "diamond"—consists of the infield and the outfield. The diamond is formed by the placement of bases (including home plate) at four corners. The object of the game is to put players "on bases" and score runs by crossing home plate.

The baseball diamond is formed by the baselines. At the center of the infield is the pitcher's mound; beyond the infield is the outfield grass.

While organized baseball is played mostly by boys, there are no rules that say girls can't join in the fun. In fact, any girl who wants to test her baseball skills playing with and against boys is welcome to try out.

Baseball is the only game in which the offensive team—the team "at bat" can't touch the ball. If a batter or baserunner does touch the ball, he or she will be ruled out.

Some girls prefer softball as an alternative.

PITCHING

The key player on the defensive team—the team in the field—is the pitcher. Standing on a slightly **elevated** "mound," the pitcher puts the ball into play and tries to keep the opponent from hitting the ball. Pitches are called strikes or balls by the **umpire**, depending on whether they are in the strike zone.

The strike zone is an invisible rectangular box the width of home plate. It extends from the batter's knees to the letters on the front of his uniform.

Pitchers grip the ball with and against the seams to change the way the ball moves. A curve ball approaches the batter in an arcing path with slightly less pace. A fastball comes more directly and with more **velocity**. A change-up looks like a fastball in the delivery, but travels more slowly.

In order to avoid injuries, young pitchers should resist trying too many trick pitches (curves, sliders, etc.) until their muscles and tendons are properly developed.

A pitcher gets more power into his pitch from his legs than from his arms.

BATTING

Batting is an **essential** part of the game. Few skills are as hard as hitting one round object (the ball) with another rounded surface (the bat). The first rule is to keep your eye on the ball from the moment it leaves the pitcher's hand until it makes contact with your bat.

There are three major parts to a good swing. They are the stride, the swing, and the follow-through. As you swing, shift your weight forward. Keep your hands high and bring the bat around, driving through the ball. After making contact, keep your head still and finish the swing.

This batter has excellent position: hands back, head still, eyes on the ball.

Your hands should be together on the handle of the bat.
Hold the bat firmly, but try to relax. When you bring the
bat around, keep the elbow of your
bottom hand tucked close to
your body. Your arms and
hands should form a "V"
as you make contact.

*Before the pitch comes, the
batter has his weight on his back
foot. When he swings at the ball,
he will shift his weight forward.*

The follow-through is very important. It finishes the swing and **ensures** all your energy and power have been fully delivered through the bat to the ball. If you chop at the pitch and don't follow through, you won't be able to generate maximum power.

Home run king Barry Bonds has a sweet swing and a sweeter follow-through.

When swinging the bat, the golden rule is to keep your head still. With a pitch coming at you hard and fast, your focus can mean the difference between a base hit and a strike-out.

When picking a bat, choose carefully. Experiment during practice to see what works best. The most important factors are comfort and bat speed. You can hit the ball farther using a light bat and quick hands than you will with a heavy bat you can't swing.

Concentration means one thing: watching the ball from the moment it leaves the pitcher's hand to the instant it makes contact with your bat.

THE CATCHER

Even though the pitcher is often the star of the team, the catcher is the boss on the field. In organized games, the catcher "calls the pitches," which means signaling the pitcher to throw a curve ball or a strike. The catcher must be a good, strong, durable athlete.

The catcher is always on hand to run the show and help with the defensive side of the game.

For protection, catchers wear a variety of equipment. This includes a helmet and face mask. Also, the catcher straps on shin guards and a thick chest pad to protect against foul balls. A protective jock and cup is **mandatory** for all ballplayers.

Catchers' masks are made of lightweight materials.

Ironically, the gear a catcher wears is called "the tools of ignorance" because catching is a thankless job. But the catcher is usually a very smart player who knows the game very well.

Because of **aluminum** bats, catchers don't have to worry about being struck by broken bats. However, they do have to worry about being run over by baserunners trying to score at home plate.

The catcher and the home plate umpire spend the whole game together.

FIELDING

In addition to the pitcher and catcher, there are seven defensive positions. They are first, second, and third base, shortstop (between second and third), and the three outfielders: left, right, and center field. Infielders must always be ready, have their knees bent, gloves open, and their eyes on the ball.

Getting low on a grounder is a good idea, so it won't skitter between your feet.

To catch an infield grounder correctly, let the ball roll into your outstretched glove, then trap it with your throwing hand. Outfielders taking fly balls should hold their glove high and keep their throwing hand near the mitt. If you bobble the ball, you may have a second chance to trap it.

This outfielder shows perfect form shagging fly balls.

Infielders who snare ground balls and make quick relays to throw out runners use a slightly smaller glove than their teammates in the outfield. On the other hand, outfielders make better use of bigger gloves to make running catches on fly balls that might otherwise be out of reach.

The first baseman's mitt is different than other infielders' gloves. It has a flat side and looks like a crab claw. The flat side helps the fielder catch throws in the dirt.

Infielders must be skilled at catching the ball and quickly throwing it to first base.

BASERUNNING

Another important element of baseball and softball is baserunning. A batter becomes a baserunner the moment contact is made with the ball. On a ground ball to one of the infielders, the batter must sprint to first base. If he beats the relay from the infielder, the runner earns an infield hit.

If a batted ball clears the infield, the batter should run to first base while watching to see how the ball is played by the outfielder. The runner may "round" first base and head toward second. If the ball is fielded cleanly, the runner retreats to first base. If not, the runner may advance.

Speed can help any batter stretch a single into a double.

Baserunners can be caught off base if they're not careful. If a runner on first base doesn't reach second base before a relay, he is forced out. If he runs on a fly ball and can't get back after the putout is made and before the ball is relayed to the fielder at that base, he's out.

Baserunners may "lead off" a base. This means taking a couple of steps toward the next base. But a runner can only do so once the pitcher has delivered. If the ball gets away from the catcher, the runner may attempt to advance. This is called stealing.

First base is the only base a runner may "overrun" to beat a throw from one of the infielders. If the runner "rounds" the base, however, he or she may be tagged out.

One of the most exciting plays is when a baserunner is caught between bases, and the defensive team has to chase him down and tag him out.

THE UMPIRES

Most youth baseball games call for two umpires (referees) on the field. One stands behind home plate and wears a mask and chest protector like the catcher. His job is to call balls and strikes. His partner stands near second base and makes the calls on infield plays at the bases. Together they ensure that this exciting game is fairly played by both sides.

The home plate umpire has the hardest job in the game. On every single pitch—ball or strike—somebody will disagree with his call and probably let him know it.

The umpire doesn't care who wins, only that the game is played fairly.

GLOSSARY

aluminum (ah LOO muh num) — a silvery-white metallic element

elevated (EL uh vayt ed) — raised above a given level

ensures (en SHOORZ) — to make positive

essential (ee SEN chul) — something that is necessary; basic

mandatory (MAN duh tor ee) — something required by law or rules

umpire (UHM pie er) — a referee or judge hired to rule on plays

velocity (vuh LOS it ee) — rate of speed

Further Reading

Bernard, Andy. *Seven Steps to Pitching.* Pleasant Word, 2003

Fitzgerald, Ron. *Baseball: Becoming a Great Hitter.* Children's Press, 2000

Fitzgerald, Ron. *Baseball: Fielding Ground Balls.* Children's Press, 2000

Wyman, Janet, et.al. *Baseball for Everyone: 150 Years of America's Game.* Harry N. Abrams, Inc., 2003

Websites to Visit

Baseball Links @ www.baseball-links.com/

Baseball Reference @ www.baseball-reference.com

Baseball America @ www.baseballamerica.com/today

Major League Baseball @ www.mlb.com

Index

About the Author

Morgan Hughes is the author of more than 50 books on hockey, track and field, bicycling, and many other subjects. He lives in Connecticut with his wife, daughter, and son.